THE SMELL OF CAMPFIRE

Poems by
KG Newman

ALSO BY KG NEWMAN

While Dreaming of Diamonds in Wintertime
(2013)

Selfish Never Get Their Own (2016)

Husband Father Failure (2019)

©2022 by KG Newman

HIDDEN PEAK
P R E S S

Published by Hidden Peak Press
November 24, 2022
Parker, Colorado
HiddenPeakPress.com | @HiddenPeakPress

IBSN 978-1-959680-00-0

Manufactured in the United States of America
Cover Art: RJ Sangosti
Author Photograph: Justin Rampy

Proudly sold at Tattered Cover Colfax
Denver, Colorado

For my kids: Bel, Jax & Bo.

CONTENTS

I &
FATHERHOOD PAST

II &
FATHERHOOD PRESENT

III ♣
FATHERHOOD UNFULFILLED

IV ♣
FATHERHOOD FUTURE

THE SMELL OF CAMPFIRE

Poems by
KG Newman

I ♣ FATHERHOOD PAST

Three snowflakes for every black chip of soot
we send into the sky.
And he can feel the snow always

falling, my father, who orders me to ready the fire.

— from "Bonfire" by Ryan Vine, 2016

ANTITWILIGHT

I love and fear sunsets
with my son; I run east while still
looking west, too slow
to ditch inevitable shadows.

Eventually snow will come
and he knows
I hide from that too,
desperate for ballgames

to continue as I search
for more time, more light,
scorekeeping the intangibles
of our sky's pink and purples.

The answers require meditation
and thousands of renegade details
tied together tightly with yarn,
as if fatherhood is a bundle of sticks

to toss on the future fire
selectively, as the late autumn
breeze comes in and an old man
needs a little warmth.

GROWING UP GIVING UP HOMERS

My mother paid someone else
to be my mother. My father felt
teaching the splitter
was sufficient enough. He said
if I ever wonder why my pitch
is too straight,
it's a mystery of proximity.
Spread my fingers further
from the laces. Ask the au pair
to take me to practice
and on the way envision
success in the streaks
out a highway window.
Whatever's bothering me,
put it off. Remember
this spin is proprietary.
No, my hand is not
turning into a hologram.

THE UNDERCURRENT

Being a big believer in
the spiritual significance of drywall,
I stood with my son in the July heat
at the razing of my old elementary
and cried buckets.

The waterworks weren't the reason
I can't explain to him how
sitting crows are unaffected
by power lines or why
I've been relying on beer
to reveal my history's hieroglyphics
along with several tall glasses
of morning ice water
to decipher them entirely.

As this pandemic wanes after claiming
grandpas and schools and breweries
I need another one to take its place
and remind me of the isolated smell
of my young son's hair, like
I've never eaten a strawberry before.

CUTLINES

The Babe keeps walking out of my closet
in the middle of the night,
with my vision set to sepia
and my hands tattooed
in varying shades of newspaper ink.
He tells me the keys to beating the Beast
and while I could guess who I'll be in decades,
I'd rather love so deeply
in the dark of the moment
that I fear the loss
          of my son's paragraph on whales
the day it's written in kindergarten,
full of beautiful phonetic spellings
that I immediately put behind glass.
I fingerprint him weekly. I keep following
The Babe's advice, documenting the evolving
strength of calves' spiracles, reading ahead
while gripping the past, everything lost
to unavoidable obsolescence
somehow found again
          while chewing my cigar.

AVOIDING GRAVITY

The truth lies where I can trip on it:

The search for the selfish gene
leads me into my old basement
where my father keeps his rapiers

and meanwhile, my ex-wishes pace
in the shadows of the attic,
learning certain foreign words and accents

to soften harsher news coming.
I fill the pool with rum and cover the drive
in yoga mats. I become an enigma

in the future recall memory of my son.
When this is all done my hands are
cut, but empty, as I leave covered in mud

imagining myself as a hawk above.

INVENTORY

I've spent all winter figuring out
what I have been trying to tell myself,

playing snow baseball with ghosts
who don't know what year it is,

the exit sign I inherited from my father
flickering in clouds a red-tailed hawk

keeps cutting through. We see
each other, but neither of us move.

Finally it flies to where the ball
blends with the white sky, and where

when I pull to open the atmosphere,
all eclipses disappear. Spoken plumes

become part of my ethos. Short
on sharp air, but I'm breathing fine.

Realizing everything but my son
and the mountains around me

I could do without, fixing this old
ripped glove, zip-tying my wrists.

IGNORING THE EQUINOX

I'm doing laundry on a warship,
drying my button-downs
on the halyard, laying onesies
over the cannons. This gives me
time to learn the names of birds
and catch my mind in its web
when the oysters are tasting
like strawberries again.
In this aching waning summer
of tentative silences, my son
builds new constellations
up there, next to where
my grandfather is walking
and talking with my father,
giving a brief history
of personal oncology while
still searching for their mitts.
I know it's not too late
for my own penance.
A dusted-off natal chart
as a good start. Tonight's stars
a skein of inferences again
to remind me who I am.

MY FATHER'S LATE NIGHTS

Flipping between Leno and Letterman,
ironing his shirts in his boxers
by the glow of far-away soundstages,

periodically walking a few feet
from the board to the bed
to close my eyes with his hand
and tell me there's a hundred bricks
all over my body – *Your arms
are feeling verrrry heavy*

and suddenly they do,
overcome with comforting weight
as I listen to the cymbal crash
and the crowd laughing

and my dad uttering a chuckle
every now and then, between
wrinkles becoming more permanent
the harder and harder he presses.

WATER IN MY LUNGS

I've never camped with my dad
and I keep all my regrets
on the shelf in my coat closet,
in boxes with little color-coded tags

while I think of contrails as
untied shoelaces and I somehow
lose my desire to kill spiders
right as I'm trying to buy a pumpkin

but used car prices are at
an all-time high, and jazz is
no longer fashionable, and our back door
is still missing its handle. Yet lost

in the panic, I find nostalgia
in my grip. We watch birds nosedive
into pools, believing they, too, are scheming
to get with Wendy Peffercorn.

OUR ENDANGERED RARITY

When the wheat grew tall enough
to recall the moment we'd changed,
and we could finally admit it,
was a few months after
I drew a squiggly line in the sand
to protect against the time goblins
and I kept re-drawing it
each thirty seconds, after the sea
washed it away at our feet.
In this way the price of bullets
does correspond to marital conflict,
as does the rising admission
at the kids' favorite pumpkin patch
which is destined to be burned soon,
after steam from the funnel cake machine
wafts into the sky to take the form
of various predators above us,
first a tigress then a lion
then an anthropomorphic liger
begging us to hold our fire.

THE COOLING OF SUMMER

The flies disappear earlier
than normal and in come clouds
that cannot be trusted,
as if these seasonal nosebleeds
are propaganda
for our personal war
or there is a white bear somewhere
in search of her infrared honey.

We sit around in silence, waiting
for tips of the trees to turn brown.
Every morning the price
for a clear mind rises
and our son's cauliflower ear
hardens, the way
we fight for something
solely out of principle:

I remember my father
stalking autumn's last flies
with a rolled-up paper,
regret in his swat before
he got on his living room floor
to show me escape moves
and the intuition to
the only love he knew.

PINECONES

This is the autumn
of tentative truths:
Excuse the kompromat
in my wife's possession
and try to understand
how stubborn love
can explain this family
as a steady-state theory.
Like how my son's
current arm slot

is the same as mine
in 1995, when I too
searched for my curve
and my father set clocks
five minutes forward.
He'd only eat chicken
in turducken and leaves
were signals to him.
He referred to them as
the DNA of hope.

II ♠ FATHERHOOD PRESENT

With the smell of my son's hair
vacuum-sealed in a vial, deep within my palm,
I start up the mountain

at sunrise. My beard has outgrown fear.
Once I summit, I'll hold my breath until
this fire turns blue.

EATING ROSEBUDS

If it's not the campfire it's the roses,
if it's not the roses it's the pinetar
and sunflower seeds: Every sniff
of every day I forget to take
doesn't have to be a play at the plate
but I'm fighting it feeling like it,

like a West Coast playoff game
keeping me up late in angst only to wake
bleary-eyed in the morning, unable to recall
who won as I find a scathing self-review
waiting in a neat stack on my desk.

There, clearly, in red ink, is an indictment
not yet ruled on by the high courts:
It says there's still time for me
to change. To recognize the moment
as the memory in the moment.
To push my son on the swing

without counting down the minutes
until he can pump himself.
If we do happen to pass roses on the way home
I'll probably let him prick his thumb then
stop the dripping nonchalantly, with a glob
of tar. Probably medicate with s'mores

a little later, but I'm not
thinking about that yet.
I'm focused on trying to enjoy this,

please, I'm just doing my best
to watch the game with my son and ignore
the quiet shadows mock-drafting the results
of different outcomes of myself.

BLOOM

I'm counting on my son
to help me break
the curse, so I've been
casually training him
for this moment
by memorizing
an index of cliff ruins
and the quickest ways
to descend a staircase.

In this Styrofoam Kingdom
he's growing up in,
he'll fashion self-motivations
for putting his beer down
and kicking it back too,
after the tallgrass
is shriveled by winter's tears
and some other cubs wonder
where their father is.

AMNESTY

I become a bike, I measure everything,
emerge among scarecrows
to define loyalty by a flag's tatters
and present parallelograms of light.
Are we back to the point where
we're okay to be afraid?
Like feeling the ripeness of apples
as an exercise in patience.
Climbing waterspouts just to prove
we can still defy phenomena.
This isn't a movie voiceover anymore,
it's the sound of trainers on gravel
by our son's first velocipede:
Shining red like a cut, with
a loud, high-pitched horn.
He can't say he didn't warn us.
We are not short on circles.

WHITEWATER

Again it's the longest day of the year.
I take Papa's photo albums down
to the riverbank as part of my investigation
into when people made the switch
to living in color. Kids race scooters
on the path in front of my bench,
avoiding a double helix of pebbles.
I think back to a pair of mitts
cracked and dusty in my father's garage.
I keep this overthinking up
and I might have to take out a loan,
become a lawyer. It's one thing
for the river to smell different
but now the dirt does, too.
Plus there are less animals in the clouds,
more ambiguity. Each page of frames
leads to more questions like Why
is there a claviharp in the background?
I imagine my own instrument here
and let the notes bounce off the water,
pour more mead, feel hard at nothing.
I lose count of the amount of dream teeth
I spit into my hand.
It must be something from my childhood
that makes it painful for me
to pay for flowers or has me wondering
where the fire escape is
when I get to the pic of everyone
crowded around Papa's last birthday cake.
One day soon we'll all appreciate

one of the old jazz standards
and not have to worry about any of this.
Her, me, everyone we love, on the porch,
adults content with themselves
and the choices we've made, eating
peaches from various positions,
reading Nietzsche from when he was sick.

CHOOSING YOU AGAIN

I watch a silent film about divorce
and am forced to imagine
the pleas the children are making.

Outside, you water potted sunflowers
with all the puddles
that split our grip on various walks.

You've denied this sort of confessional before.
Earlier, outside the bank,
we ran into a con man

who claimed we'd be rich
if we just focused on the unhappiness
of three other couples.

But even that con man
had tattered shoes and soon he too
will be shaving without a mirror

right outside a marbled bathroom,
somewhere in the near future,
as we remember this day

and all the birds chirp encouragement
at the strong, stubborn lovers
still hanging on.

FINDING MY SMALL ACT

Have you ever seen a superhero
with a gun? I can't be certain because I keep
looking away when the villains come

kind of like watching all nine seasons
of the classic American comedy
but not the emotional finale —

the implications being I accelerate
at just the right moment around sharp corners,

I fly by the old men sweeping
their sidewalks, who smile and wave
instead of gesturing to slow down:
So something is different about today.

The fonts, maybe. The pines mistaken
for bulletproof cover. An infant lynx
stretching in open tallgrass leading to

my finest accomplishment yet:
Leaving a mixing bowl of milk
on the porch this morning
and seeing it dry by lunch.

THE PREVENTION OF ROBOTS

While letting out a long, primal scream
at my email I wonder if there's any way
to permanently shut off all the screens
in my purview, and my children's,
and in every room and building

we enter. Impossible goal you're likely
thinking. True. Snipping the power lines
won't do. Neither will re-introducing
conversation techniques and the epistle
in schools, or unearthing
millions of miles of cables.

So I aim my grandfather's .22 at the satellites,
wherever they might be in the fiber-optic sky.
I instruct my son to hold my beer
and remind him, in an evolving memory,
the best way to hurt your eyes
is staring into the sun.

EMOTIONAL BOOTSTRAPPING

When I finally summon the guts
to sweep the dead moths
from the red barn for my son
with thousands of carcasses
shoved off into the tallgrass
and the dust catching sunlight
streaming through
the propped doors,
it's half bliss
and half-sneezing brutality
as I survey the nails
coming through the roof
and run my finger along
a rusted one
just to see if it can cut.

A HUNDRED DIFFERENT VERSIONS
OF MY SON

I keep my son's baby teeth
in a jar in my desk drawer

next to the ziploc of clippings
from his first haircut.

I frame his genesis paragraph
and make it the refrain of my dreams.

Carve his every made-up portmanteau
into the tallest tree out back.

Our secret handshakes
become the only currency

and I curse myself for not journaling
his all-time height relative to our favorite cloud

because infinite rolls of film will never
be enough. I need the temperature

of the sun on his face at six. The smell
of every vacation with him, bottled.

I need a hundred different versions
of my son when I close my eyes, on loop

at various ages, all the knee scrapes
and one-liners my mind can't contain.

I tell him this theory one afternoon
driving home from school

while asking about his day for details
I'll speak into my recorder later,

fatherhood being a skein of vortices
I need his help collecting.

THANKSGIVING AT THE PLAYGROUND

My son is glue and my daughter is water
as I climb the slide with my eyes closed
in search of my wife.

Logs spin while we run and jump;
the ball for four square has just
enough air. Every head bump on some bar

is a memory I'll run my hand over later,
with thinning hair and worst-case papers
still unsigned in front of me.

These are the lovely insecurities that come
of an unseasonably warm late November,
before the temperature drop

and along with repentant woodchips
in our socks, everything wrong with us
turning out to be a sinus problem.

MAGNUS EFFECT

My son squares his attention
with a barrel. Crushed buckets
of feelings, stinging my pitches
like retribution, doing it again.

I volunteer to shag with him —
warm leather mixing
with GLVs, regret and hope
in my nose — a moratorium
on my errors. I accept

what is concluded
these afternoons when two
opposing forces come together —
I always slip the furthest hit
in my pocket. A father, yes,
and also a little bit helpless.

THE SKY IS FAT

Among the naked branches
my heart is a type of bark.

I give legitimacy to clouds and
the same fatherhood that happens

to me happens to them.
Sunlight is passed down

into our bones and accumulations
of silhouetted moments

gain heat as light creeps
low behind the mountains and

I am low-brimmed, determined
cowboys digging a fire pit

in a hard earth reverberating;
we are their smoky ballads

written in the meter of seeds.

TREASURE

Everything in 8-bit, and with
an implication. Gator on the green.
Blue heron on the gator's back,
selling recall from under
a ten-gallon hat.

From above, it could be a watercolor
by you in another life.
You painted it after
a fight with your father,
climbing the big maple
and staying there while
the flies established themselves
in the house for good that summer.
A long, hot June just like this one,

with rows of putts in front of you.
Only this time you tell your son
to grab the brush
and trust his line to the gator's mouth.
The ball stops short
and at half-peace

but you'll take it just the same,
having finally remembered the sand trap
where the koseki is buried.

MAINTENANCE INSOMNIA

There's a chance it's a boo hag —
fractional, I admit, but still —
as I ruled out my son
recently getting lost at the beach
in his spin on the Wendy Peffercorn ploy
and the humidity wicking my soul
while I swing and I think
from a three-hundred-year-old tree.

What I need is a blueprint of the wharf
tattooed atop my forearm.
This will also help me
when running past the Bohemian Hotel
on River Street, in versions
of myself, and in predawn negotiations
with the statue of the waving girl.

I need my intentions brick-paved,
and an attractive dilapidated.
I want to know the truth
when I lay awake at night.
I want my own cable-stayed bridge
to ride into a brief stay in the sky.

PAUSING FATHERHOOD

My son is now 45 pounds but I swear
he's half as light as the same plate
I have in my garage gym:
I lift him up using just my back.
I hoist him unlimited times over my head
and toss him effortlessly onto the laundry pile
on the bed. Meanwhile in my workouts
the fatigue slaps me
after a few tracks and lackluster sets.
There is no substitute for dad strength,
besides the much-desired mom strength.
To summon it I say his name
when doing crunches. I memorize the smell
of his hair over planks. In the corner
there's a 70-pound dumbbell gathering dust,
wondering why it's taking so long
for me to pick it up like air,
like the weight he'll be
in three more short years.
The exertion makes me elated and tired
all at once and in need
of the naps my father used to take,
sleeping with his forearm over his eyes
as if preparing to ward off the sun.

III ♠ FATHERHOOD UNFULFILLED

My wounds are potholes on streets
amid the tallest buildings.
I can't tell if it's cold out or if the steam

is from some faraway fire,
ignited by poultices filled
with flowers lost and misidentified.

EMPTY SPACE

Since then, molasses creeps down the hill
threatening to overrun our village.

The anchors wonder if time still matters
while she keeps bleeding in the bathroom.

Every dream we had for our son's brother
exists in constellations now, and

we're not running out of rockets but rather
other planets to feel sad on.

So we stack sandbags around the house
and stock up on waffles. I use my last fuel

on the lawn and crumple all the dollars
I have left. Finally I stop asking her

if she needs coffee. I just turn on the pot,
spill the sugar, and weep.

CICATRIX

Sitting lost again in rush hour traffic
I like to pretend I'm someone who doesn't
check my email all the time
and that I could tell you with certainty
how the downtown streets were named.

In this way improvisational history
is also the history of us, a confusion
that only agreed to be with clarity
if our kids could hold both our hands
while skipping to the roller coaster.

We've debated the exact half-life
of stars above us, though
no agreement has been reached.
And she keeps reminding me we have many
types of knives, each capable of making
exactingly shallow cuts like

the feeling we're losing something
and gaining it back all the same,
the static between the buildings,
an abandoned, ivied train station where
there's no need for waiting anymore.

LOOKING FOR HIS BROTHER

I drive around on perpetual low gas
and listen to jazz which
I substituted for coffee at three
as a soundtrack to jamming
on the Little Tikes hoop;
Now these same standards
put my son to sleep
on the ride home from kindergarten
even if I still don't know
what one thing
I'm grabbing out the door
in a fire, before the scenario where
we need to peel to a stop in front
of a rafter of turkeys crossing the road.
I'm still trying to figure out
what I can learn from reading
disclaimers on cereal boxes,
mornings after I walk
out his bedroom door the night before
while thinking of something
temporarily left ajar,
like sun streaking in transom windows
on a warming, late winter day.

ANNUAL DUE DATE

The winter sunlight exposes
window smudges and
dusty countertops, and later

snow falls so slowly
it appears to be rising
in the moonlight, like

something I'm unaware of
still governing me
and causing arrhythmia,

an apology always on the tip
of my tongue and problems
with verisimilitude

buried deep while she stands
in the forest with just-washed hair,
understanding loss,

waving above with her hand
a speck of a speck and my son
of a hundred years ago

using a finger gun to tell me
to put my heart in the bag so
the hurt can find a purpose.

WAITING ON ANOTHER

I called the hospital:
Is she out of surgery yet?
In response the nurse
faxed me a cryptic acrylic
of hieroglyphic blood drops
across monochrome tile
with no discernible pattern.

Since then I've charted
the inertia of the twilights
and the flight speed
necessary for infant birds.
I've been tinkering with
the perfect formula. Adding
various strands of her hair

while she takes buckets
of halved baby aspirins,
mutters a list of names
as she sleeps. I prefer
the ones that remind me
of looming castles,
warm skin, actual cement.

BEST INTENTIONS

My folks bring over a shrub
as an offering for what we lost.
My dad says *When we miscarried,*
Papa bought us a tree,
but you probably have
enough trees. So here's
this shrub, planted with loneliness
in an empty bed
in front of our farmhouse
in the forest. I wonder if it will be safe
where the dogs can get it
and my wife says it will be
even though we both know
that's a lie. Similar to why
two weeks ago we stopped believing
in gardens. Suddenly the gnomes
seemed anti-hope. And three weeks
from tomorrow, we'll come home
to the last mangled, chewed roots
strewn across the lawn.
I'll look up at the trees
wanting to give up and thinking
about ribboned blood
in the toilet, your pale skin,
the doctor speaking and
my mind leaving him on mute.
I'll kick dirt back into the hole,
wish for a two-story pine.
The dogs will have our grief
unearthed again by morning.

SEARCHING FOR FULL

We put the skeleton under our bed
and turn off the water.
The hope is for a succession
of slightly overcast days
with a wind robust enough
to carry our love down the line.
The reality is brutally oppressive heat,
verbal abuse, the shrub
we planted in the front
as some consolation memory
now wilted and sad
like the funk we've been
running from. Soon
I believe some cereal
will wake us up: One huge bowl
for both of us, mostly milk,
the oats all half-dissolved.

CARRYING MY LIBRARY CARD

We take the two-lane road
to the lie-berry, as my son dubs it,
the wind fierce and pushing
birds in and out of open spaces
as we drive. My daughter sits
shotgun. The empty car seat

is still in back, beside him.
We talk about the books
we might get, but never the one
we know is still unavailable.
The winter sky is bright
with smoke clouds looming
to the north. Who knew

we'd still be dealing with wildfires
in January? My daughter points out
some flames never go away.
With snow bowing branches
it can stay inside stacks of hay

in our barn, waiting for a steady
drip onto the bales, sparking in
the middle of the night as I'm
dreaming of a younger him again.

FREEZING THE BEARING

The day it snowed in Death Valley
all the fruit trees in our neighborhood
came to, as if it was the last great
harvest left. Even when I walked

the dog, it needed to be zig-zagged,
like that would prolong sharp feelings
from absorbing into my bloodstream.

In this way I'm certain there are aliens
watching with reverse telescopes and
I am still duped by all official-looking
junk mail, while boldly holding out hope
in the crayoned schematics I act on:

A stick figure family for comfort,
folded neatly in my pocket. Walking
surprisingly mean suburban streets
with thinned tennis shoes I sharpied
with hers and the kids' red initials.

RENDERINGS OF A SCAR

My late son, in my version of heaven,
is reading the box scores aloud
with his Cheerios or beef jerky. Now
he ponders the standings. No.
He is listening for his mom, below
in the kitchen. Is she laughing hard
or still crying? These fleeting answers
only come when bounding down
a flight of stairs, or looking lost

on a corner among skyscrapers.
I'd tell him to eat up because
he can't miss the bus again and that
my love for him is like sand spanned
across the quiet breakfast tables
of minted time. The sound of grit from
just moving the butter. Chewing loudly
while believing he's always been
like me, learning under lintels.

US AGAIN

It wasn't until we built the playset
that I knew we would be okay.
A thousand boards bolted into place.
Me drilling into the high beams
while you read from the booklet
propped up on your belly.
I guess we just needed pilot holes.
No sense in all that splintering
and we finally set a realistic pace,
used some loose dirt to make
our own version of flat.
When we got done I lit a match
to remember the smell of how we were
and then we drove around the county
debating the purpose of every fence.
Livestock? Aesthetic? A barrier
or a gateway to a runaway field
growing herbs just for poultices?

IV ♠ FATHERHOOD FUTURE

While organizing my son's action figures by the fire
I imagine the father each of them could be:

like at what age Bruce Wayne
lets his son climb behind the wheel
to disregard lane lines across Gotham,

in the morning the never-ending lampblack tracks
juxtaposing this mansion of light.

THE SMELL OF CAMPFIRE

I take my receipts of scar tissue
and trudge through the snow
for more little sticks, disfigured
branches, sprigs of
dry dead pine needles.

This is the fragile conviviality
I envision, my grown sons and I
roasting mallows in the dark,
recuperating faith with fistfuls
of untreated lumber.

To our yellow-orange faces I say
to sacrifice me to the weather
if it comes to that. Hopefully
it won't but they both know
how disproportions creep in

and the campfire requires
a pale-knuckle grip on its memory,
as if the sparks can bark out
colors of coming sunrises or
our uncertainties in disguise.

THE FEAR OF BLANK FACES

I'm relying on sweepstakes
to bring me back my happiness
and the panic from future mismemories
to get this addiction under control.

Hence stepping into
simulacrums of our house —
a giant cardboard box, a chicken coop —
as a preventative measure to make sure
I can still categorize all my son's birthdays

and in the way our city's jagged steel buildings
are privately owned but spiritually public,
I walk along a route of long-demolished
ballparks, now serving as banks and

parking lots, and spray paint a white plate
at each approximated spot. I imitate the swing
of a ballplayer I do not know. I can only
make out my wife's hair,
waving in the stands.

THINKING ABOUT ASTERISKS

Pete Rose is lying again:
He's going around the supermarket
saying he's in the Hall of Fame:
and in-between picking apples with my son
I cough in affirmation.

Who gives? I like a feint
of gold in my water.
I don't mind rain on a sunny day.
And there's no way to tell me
obsession doesn't come with

a bit of superstition in posterity:
Rose says his record could be broken
but he's not counting on it. Then he grins,
and pays for beer and scratch cards
with a large bag of pennies.

UNDER MY FINGERNAILS

Fueled by aging parents
selling my childhood home
plus totaling my trusty rusting truck
the very next morning,
I set out this Monday determined,
and with fresh hunger:

Biting the heads off
my string cheese. Chewing on ice,
canceling my insurance.
The more the city's concrete hardens,
the more I become unsettled,
determined to stop the moon

from the gutter of the street.
Gambling on the weather a thing of the past.
Total control is the only currency now.
Scarred hands glinting while
chopping wood, treehousing with

my son, burying his bunny. Everything else
is Astroturf and balls bouncing
unnervingly high, up into the empyrean.
I spit into my glove. I am ready
to be buried in dirt.

THE FUTURE WE INHERIT

My dad always grumbles about gas stations
charging for air like my grandfather did,
before he walked along ponds in Zen
with a scooper at sunset, mining
for premium golf balls.

He had boxes of them when cancer called
and they ended up in a stack in our garage,
a few feet from my dad's front tire
slowly leaking at its seam.
He'd drive on it as long as he could

before needing to refill. *We've all got
oscillating feelings,* he'd explain as
the wheels turned to another game
and the urn moved
further back along the road.

Now when I drive around, wondering why
I'm still slicing all my drives, I can't place
where he's buried exactly
but I can imagine as I pass churches
up and down Broadway

like picturing the small two-story brick house
where he was born in north Denver,
across from the microbrewery
my dad and I frequent
on the walk to the ballpark.

As the innings move along and my son knows
the quirks of his grandfather,
sidewalks are the origin story
and the dusty boxes become
coffers in my memory:

I considered using ancestral DNA
to identify the gruff gene,
but met with birds instead.
I googled my grandfather's full name.
Couldn't find a thing.

ALLIANCE

Fatherhood seeds the reign of vulnerability:
Steel-toe boots demand calloused but open
palms, and the never-ending inning birthed
a gritty bullpen. They've tweaked the mound
but it's always been like this. Fortunately,
when clouds look like liger cubs, a maple tree
can become a barrel, and is our son waiting to
learn a launch angle previously undiscovered.
I'll remain perpetually short of declaring war.
Boiling rapids for him, downriver from
someone humming Vivaldi.

TRANSMITTING HAPPINESS FROM
THE CUSP OF EXTINCTION

My son draws the future
while I wait for water to boil.
Catastrophic climate change
has brought us the longest
Indian summer ever.
He's using the black crayons
down to their nubs. The clouds
are disturbingly low, yellowish.
He tapes the construction paper
to the fridge. *We'll see if*

they can deny this, he declares.
But what's the fairness
in a predetermined fate?
So I press for another tableau,
this one of our family
picnicking with gas masks on
in the woods, with
an occasional endangered bee
buzzing over and needing

to be waved away.
Wistful light filtering
between bare pine trees.
Him and me alternating
holding a frayed ball,
practicing our favorite grips.

THE PROPERTIES OF WAX

The hangman hands me a crayon
and gives me five minutes to scribble
the best advice I can remember
for my son. I leave out the rules
about buying a gremlin
and don't mention the benefits
of library cards in multiple counties
but I do include the news
of what I felt when I finally
found the courage
to stand on the dock
where I first kissed his mom
to watch ships dip over the horizon,
particles disappearing
into the same unforgiving sun
I'm about to stare into,
beyond the promise
of contrails and this crayon
which I crush into my palm
after signing *love Dad*,
undecided on whether
the next me
would make what's left
into a vigil candle or, alternatively,
a sealing wax for more letters.

REASONS TO STAY

Thinking of *No* as the first word
in a long and hard conversation,

trying not to be the sort of epistolarian
who can't bother to spell out *and,*

focusing on my wife's lips
in *apocalyptic*

and yes *clandestine*
somehow still reminds me of *clementine*

and the sweet sticky juice
we tried to distill on the sill

of the basement window,
hoping for an alcohol content

that would take away our anger
or perhaps get as deep as this, where

parenting words have new meanings
and fewer counterpoints.

FINDING THE RABBIT

When baseball wasn't thrilling enough
for my son — he wonders how a sport
can get by on nearly nostalgia alone —
we took up falconry together.

But first we had to stake out the land,
then cut down the power lines.
Find a reliable source of small game.
Block out a decade for the raptor
to grow with his wrists.

We put in that time and we honored
the Mongols, even got the proper permits,
but one day it took off in search
of a rabbit, and never came back.

By then my son was his own man
as he scanned the horizon for his bird
every night for a year, and then
twenty, until finally his son
came pulling on his untied jess.

FEARING FIRST GRADE

The countdown is on to the end
of kindergarten,
and with it, each day
a little piece of me dies.

This spring alone he became too cool
for holding hands
and his baby-fat habit
of grading each goodbye hug

on a firmness scale from one to one hundred.
The tighter the squeeze, the higher the number,

statistics now archived in spreadsheets
in the same brain which is glitching up

on this final May Friday, when he slings his
backpack casually over one shoulder
and declares himself

fit to walk to the front door by himself.
It's the moment all his made-up portmanteaus

see their market value increase exponentially
and when I feel my bottom front tooth wiggle

like his has been doing for weeks.
I move it around with my tongue
and I mouth his name

as he catches up to his buds,
swivels his hat backwards,
says something funny while I try

to picture him now, with all his baby teeth,
still in kindergarten, my cementum
hinging on everything.

THE SEARING

My son laughs in his sleep and
at the mall, all the stores
turned over since my childhood.

That's what I think about while
we drive through a snow squall
on the way to his school, down

county roads, nowhere near
the new-look mall. The air smells
of nutmeg. The whole horizon is

born from the alpenglow and
the antitwilight. I wonder how
honest we can all be with

each other, these passing generations,
if the white wind we inherit can't be
unfurled without this code,

the digits coming to us in the middle
of the tucked night, between lucid laughs
and micrometers of growth.

BROKEN A/C

Fatherhood is coming to terms
with your shortcomings
while listening to 103.5 The Fox
with all the windows rolled down

and your son dissecting clouds
in the back seat, also lost in thought
and also with one arm cocked out
into the street, his palm open

like yours, bottling the breeze,
taking inventory of the sky's menagerie
and saving his saving words
for the hottest day of the summer.

GENERATIONAL THIRST

I dig my son a river
which we ride until
it evaporates into dirt,
and by then we're experts
in reverse osmosis
and the raw inheritance
of unsentimentality.

All the flowers of lore
supposed to keep us young
I toss into the fire.
It's not that I don't want
to study his sleeping face
or stuff my pillows
with his old onesies:

It's just that the time lapse
of him drinking
droplets from a leaf
leaves me paralyzed
like an ant attempting
to watercolor the forest
with the few sticks gathered.

So I memorize the words
he once said beautifully incorrect.
Dry out the hides of our best baseballs.
Then we walk back up along
the crocodile-cracked river, believing
it will lead us to a stream.

SUMMONING SPARTACUS

I string up thieves by their feet just to see
what it's like to wait on them for once,
in an alley, tiptoeing around the full moon.

I commission gladiator fights into my will,
just to prove there's no logarithm for despair
and it is possible to farm in the dark.

In a previous life, en route to chariot races,
splinters of time glittered in my fist
along with sharp rocks and moon dust

from future generations' munera.
The dead will still be asking too much
as rivers flow back to their sources

and the sons of the world forge
their own armor, ready to fight and die
just to have something to believe in.

TOMORROW'S FATHERHOOD

I'll move past everything being
a series of short-term contracts
and plant a tree where the shrub
kept getting dug up.
By then I'll have a patent
on freezing antitwilights
and a thriving small business devoted
to preserving bits of old drywall.
Between silent films and small acts
and undercurrents, the sooty smoke
I camp around each wandering summer
will prove good for me, cleansing,
somehow curing my arrhythmia.
I won't have thought about the hangman
handing me a crayon in a while
and my son

will be sleeping with his forearm over his eyes,
using his mom's watermelon belly
as a pillow. It'll be close to us returning
to the ivied station.
All the trains running on time.
We'll have missed it like years since seeing
a good game at Wrigley, the pitchers
throwing splitters where they want them.
We will be ready for anything,
and she and I agree we both
weirdly find appeal in apocalyptic lips.
We can drink streamwater to survive.
Sitting around the fire, all waiting

for a boil together, and that's when
it will hit us: Say we name him Bodie,
meaning *messenger*.

ACKNOWLEDGEMENTS

Antitwilight first appeared in *Nassau Review*

Growing Up Giving Up Homers first appeared in *Sledgehammer Lit*

The Undercurrent first appeared in *Tule Review*

Avoiding Gravity and *Choosing You Again* first appeared in *West Trade Review*

My Father's Late Nights and *Alliance* first appeared in *Hidden Peak Review*

Our Endangered Rarity first appeared in *Boats Against The Current*

Empty Space first appeared in *Scapegoat Review*

Cicatrix and *Reasons To Stay* first appeared in *Miniskirt Magazine*

Annual Due Date first appeared in *Discretionary Love*

Renderings of A Scar first appeared in *Magpie Literary Journal*

The Smell of Campfire and *Properties of Wax* first appeared in *Chantarelle's Notebook*

The Fear of Blank Faces first appeared in *HASH Literary Journal*

Thinking About Asterisks first appeared in *Platform Review*

The Future We Inherit first appeared in *Brazos River Review*

Transmitting Happiness From The Cusp of Extinction first appeared in *Black Moon Mag*

ABOUT THE AUTHOR

KG NEWMAN is a fourth-generation Coloradan and sportswriter by day at *The Denver Post*. The poet lives in Hidden Village with his wife Dani and three kids, and believes there's a bit of honesty in everybody — it just takes the right woman, daughter, son or Sunday doubleheader at Coors Field in order to bring it out. In addition to hiking, camping, cycling, skiing and living out a lost dream in men's summer league baseball, he's quick to shoot in pickup hoops and always swings the driver way too hard on the back nine. He is the 2012 valedictorian of Arizona State's Walter Cronkite School of Journalism. His first three collections of poems can be purchased on Amazon. For more info and to read his latest work online, visit kgnewman.com.

www.ingramcontent.com/pod-product-compliance
Lightning Source LLC
Chambersburg PA
CBHW030852090426
42737CB00009B/1201